W9-BWF-359

CPS-MORRILL SCHOOL LIBRARY

3 4880 05000608 4   599.7 MIL
Fur and feathers

DATE DUE			

599.7
MIL
C-1

3 4880 05000608 4
Miles, Elizabeth.

Fur and feathers

CPS-MORRILL SCHOOL LIBRARY
CHICAGO PUBLIC SCHOOLS
6011 S ROCKWELL ST
CHICAGO, IL 60629

755174 02155   45258A   0001

ANIMAL PARTS

Elizabeth Miles

Heinemann Library
Chicago, Illinois

599.7
m,2
c-1 21.55

© 2003 Reed Educational & Professional Publishing
Published by Heinemann Library,
an imprint of Reed Educational & Professional Publishing,
Chicago, Illinois

Customer Service 888-454-2279

Visit our website at www.heinemannlibrary.com

All rights reserved. No part of this publication may be reproduced or transmitted in any form or by any means, electronic or mechanical, including photocopying, recording, taping, or any information storage and retrieval system, without permission in writing from the publisher.

Designed by David Oakley at Arnos Design
Originated by Ambassador Litho Ltd
Printed in Hong Kong

07 06 05 04 03
10 9 8 7 6 5 4 3 2 1

Library of Congress Cataloging-in-Publication Data
Miles, Elizabeth, 1960-
  Fur and feathers / Elizabeth Miles.
    p. cm. -- (Animal parts)
Summary: Briefly describes how the fur and feathers of various animals
differ in shape, pattern, and function.
  ISBN 1-40340-016-4 (HC), 1-40340-425-9 (Pbk)
  1. Fur--Juvenile literature. [1. Fur. 2. Feathers.] I. Title. II. Series: Miles, Elizabeth, 1960- .
  Animal parts.

  QL942 .M485 2002
  599.7'147--dc21

                              2001006756

Acknowledgments
The author and publishers are grateful to the following for permission to reproduce copyright material: BBC Natural History Unit/Chris Packham p. 24; BBC Natural History Unit/Jeff Foott pp. 13, 28; BBC Natural History Unit/Lynn M. Stone p. 15; BBC Natural History Unit/Neil Bromhall p. 29; BBC Nautral History Unit/Staffan Widstrand p. 21; Bruce Coleman pp. 17, 26; Bruce Coleman/Kim Taylor p. 18; Corbis p. 12; Digital Stock p. 30; digital vision p. 23; NHPA/Anthony Bannister p. 16; NHPA /Eric Soder p. 22; NHPA /Jany Sauvanet p. 20; NHPA /Jeff Goodman p. 19; NHPA /John Shaw p. 27; NHPA /Kevin Shafer p. 25; NHPA /Martin Harvey p. 14.

Cover photograph reproduced with permission of Powerstock Zefa.

Every effort has been made to contact copyright holders of any material reproduced in this book. Any omissions will be rectified in subsequent printings if notice is given to the publisher.

Some words are shown in bold, **like this.** You can find out what they mean by looking in the glossary.

Contents

Hair, Fur, and Feathers

Many animals have a covering of hair or feathers. People have hair. You can see the hair on people's heads, arms, and legs. Men grow hair on their faces.

Animal hair may be thin or thick, soft or rough. A coat of soft hair is often called fur. A sheep has a covering of wool. Wool is thick, curly hair.

Fur for Warmth

Coats of fur have two kinds of hair. The soft layer near the skin is called **underfur.** It keeps the animal warm. The outer layer keeps the animal dry. This reindeer's fur keeps it warm and dry.

A polar bear lives in an icy, cold place. Its thick, furry coat helps to keep it warm. It can even walk on cold ice, because it has fur on the bottom of its feet.

Long Fur and Hair

Some animals have very long coats. The outer layer of a musk oxen's fur coat is made up of many long hairs. Its coat keeps it warm and dry in the cold.

Golden lion tamarins have long coats of orange hair. They live in leafy treetops in forests. Their long, brightly-colored coats help them find each other more easily.

Fur that Changes Color

Many **mammals** grow thicker coats in the winter and then **shed** them in the summer. In winter, an Arctic fox has a thick, white coat of fur. It keeps the fox warm and helps it hide in the snow.

When the snow melts in summer, the Arctic
fox loses a lot of its white winter fur. It is
left with a thinner, darker coat. This
summer coat matches the ground.

Shapes and Patterns of Hair

The shape and pattern of an animal's hair can be very important. It sends a message to other animals. A **male** lion has a **mane** to make it look mean.

A giraffe has dark patches on its body to help it to hide. It can hardly be seen in the shadows of a tree. Giraffes need to hide from **predators** such as lions.

Sensitive Hairs

Some animals have sensitive hairs that help the animal to feel the world around it. Wombats use their **whiskers** to feel their way around.

Many **insects** have what look like hairs.
They are really sensitive **scales.** A moth
uses them to taste with its feet! The
hair-like scales tell the moth what it
has landed on.

Hairs Like Spikes

A porcupine is covered with hard, sharp hairs called quills. If under attack, the porcupine will stick up its quills and run backward to stab its enemy.

A hedgehog has a covering of spines.
These are strong, stiff hairs with sharp
tips. The hedgehog can roll up into a spiny
ball to protect itself if an enemy is near.

Feathers

Birds have a covering of feathers instead of hair. A snowy owl lives in cold snow and ice. Even its feet and beak are covered in feathers to keep it warm.

Baby birds like these ducklings have lots of soft, fluffy feathers. These soft feathers are called down. The down keeps the ducklings warm and dry.

Feathers for Flight

A condor's wings have long, flat, stiff feathers. Each feather has many tiny strands, joined to a hollow **shaft** that runs down the middle.

Birds use their feathers to fly. The feathers make the wings wide and flat. They are light but also strong. Birds either flap their wings or **soar** through the air like this condor.

Waterproof Feathers

Many birds have oily, **waterproof** feathers that do not soak up water. A pelican can dive underwater to catch fish and come up dry.

Birds that swim underwater need to stay warm. A penguin swims in icy, cold ocean water. A layer of feathers keeps its body warm and dry.

Plain or Colorful Feathers

Different birds have different colored feathers. A nightjar has feathers that match where it lives. It can sit on its nest without being seen by a **predator.**

Some birds have very colorful feathers. **Male** quetzals have beautiful, colorful feathers. They show them off to **female** quetzals.

Cleaning Hair or Feathers

Animals keep their coats clean and healthy by taking care of their hair or feathers. Cheetahs lick their fur to keep it clean. A cheetah also licks its **cub's** fur.

Birds **preen** their feathers to keep them clean and healthy for flying. A bird uses its beak to get rid of any dirt and to make sure its feathers are **waterproof.**

No Fur

Some **mammals** do not have hair or fur, but they need to keep warm. A beluga whale has a layer of fat called blubber under its skin to keep it warm.

A naked mole rat is called that because it has hardly any hair. It lives in warm places and stays underground. It does not need thick hair to keep warm.

Fact File

- Elephants and rhinoceroses have very little hair because they have thick skin and live in warm places.

- Some **mammals** make themselves look bigger by fluffing out their fur. Cats do this to frighten off other animals.

- Birds have different numbers of feathers. One bird may have as few as 940 feathers or as many as 25,000!

Cheetahs have spots on their fur. Their fur helps them hide while they hunt.

Glossary

cub   young animal, such as a cheetah or lion

female   girl or woman

insect   small animal with three main parts to its body and six legs

male   boy or man

mammal   animal that feeds its babies with the mother's milk. People are mammals.

mane   long, thick hair on the neck of animals such as lions or horses

predator   animal that hunts other animals for food

preen   how a bird keeps its feathers clean and tidy with its beak

scales   thin, flat pieces that cover animals such as fish and snakes

shaft   long, narrow part that runs down the center of a feather

shed   allow to fall off

soar   when a bird flies high without flapping its wings

underfur   layer of soft fur near the skin

waterproof   protected from getting wet

whiskers   hairs near the mouth and nose of an animal

More Books to Read

Miles, Elizabeth. *Ears*. Chicago: Heinemann Library, 2003.

Miles, Elizabeth. *Paws and Claws*. Chicago: Heinemann Library, 2003.

Miles, Elizabeth. *Tails*. Chicago: Heinemann Library, 2003.

Miles, Elizabeth. *Wings, Fins and Flippers*. Chicago: Heinemann Library, 2003.

Index